FORCES AND ENERGY

Clare Hibbert

Enslow Publishing
101 W. 23rd Street
Suite 240
New York, NY 10011
USA

enslow.com

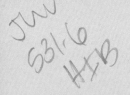

Published in 2019 by Enslow Publishing, LLC.
101 W. 23rd Street, Suite 240, New York, NY 10011

Copyright © Arcturus Holdings Ltd 2019

Cataloging-in-Publication Data

Names: Hibbert, Clare.
Title: Forces and energy / Clare Hibbert.
Description: New York : Enslow Publishing, 2019. | Series: Science explorers | Includes glossary and index.
Identifiers: ISBN 9781978506701 (pbk.) | ISBN 9781978506435 (library bound) | ISBN 9781978506763 (6pack) | ISBN 9781978506503 (ebook)
Subjects: LCSH: Force and energy—Juvenile literature. | Motion—Juvenile literature.
Classification: LCC QC73.4 H625 2019 | DDC 531'.6—dc23

Printed in the United States of America

To Our Readers: We have done our best to make sure all website addresses in this book were active and appropriate when we went to press. However, the author and the publisher have no control over and assume no liability for the material available on those websites or on any websites they may link to. Any comments or suggestions can be sent by email to customerservice@enslow.com.

Photo Credits:
Every attempt has been made to clear copyright. Should there be any inadvertent omission, please apply to the publisher for rectification.
Key: b-bottom, t-top, c-center, l-left, r-right
Alamy: CERN: 22–23 & 27br (Daniel Dominguez/Maximilien Brice); Getty Images: 16–17 (Education Images/UIG); Library of Congress: 25tr (Oren Jack Turner); NASA Images: 11cr, 20br (JPL-Caltech), 25c (ESA/Judy Schmidt), 26cr, 27bl, 28bl; Science Photo Library: 4–5 (Photo Insolite Realite), 13br, 24–25 (Nicolle R Fuller); Shutterstock: cover main & 6–7 (3Dsculptor), cover cl (Doug Lemke), cover tl & 17br (ShutterStockStudio), cover bl & 18cl & 31br (kasezo), cover tr & 23tr & 32br (GiroScience), 4tr (adriaticfoto), 4c (Neal Pritchard Media), 4br (YC_Chee), 6cr (Sombat Muycheen), 7bl (freevideophotoagency), 8–9 (Cassiohabib), 8cr (Roberto Cerruti), 8c (JonathanC Photography), 8bl (StockSmartStart), 9 cr (Aspen Photo), 10–11 (Sky Antonio), 10c (TES_PHOTO, MatiasDelCarmine, Genestro), 10bl (MatiasDelCarmine), 12–13 (Little Dog Korat), 12cl (Kosta Iliev), 12bc (pandapaw), 13tl (Morphart Creation), 14–15 (Gabor Kenyeres), 14tr (Littlekidmoment), 14c & 30br (SkyPics Studio), 14bl (Fouad A Saad), 16c (Zigzag Mountain Art), 18–19 (Kobby Dagan), 18bl (MatiasDelCarmine), 20–21 (Jag_cz), 20tr (Fouad A Saad), 21tl (ALXR), 22bl (Ayon Tarafdar), 25bl (Meowu), 26tr (Alones), 26tl (Vladimir Zhoga), 26bl (BravissimoS), 26br (Tomas Ragina), 27tl (VectorMine), 27tr (mozzyb), 27cl (Sander MeertinsPhotography), 29cr (joyfull); Wikimedia Commons: 6bl (Justus Sustermans, National Maritime Museum), 16bl (Frederick Bedell's The Principles of the Transformer (1896)), 19tr (Niabot), 29br (Natioinal Nuclear Security Administration, Nevada SIT Office).

CONTENTS

Introduction

Science is amazing! It shapes our understanding of the universe and has transformed our everyday lives. At its heart, science is a way of collecting facts, developing ideas to explain those facts, and making predictions we can test.

Laboratory Learning

Chemistry investigates materials, from solids, liquids, and gases to the tiny atoms that make up everything. By understanding the rules behind how different kinds of matter behave, we can create new chemicals and materials with amazing properties.

Scientists can observe chemical reactions under a microscope.

Secrets of the Universe

Physics is the scientific study of energy, forces, mechanics, and waves. Energy includes heat, light, and electricity. Physics also looks at the structure of atoms and the workings of the universe. Even the galaxies obey the laws of physics!

Chimpanzees are one of around 7.8 million species of living animals.

Many forms of energy are involved in a storm.

Life on Earth

Natural history is the study of living things—the countless plants, animals, and other creatures that inhabit Earth now or which existed in the past. It studies how these organisms are influenced by each other and their environment. It also looks at the complex process of evolution—gradual change from one generation to the next.

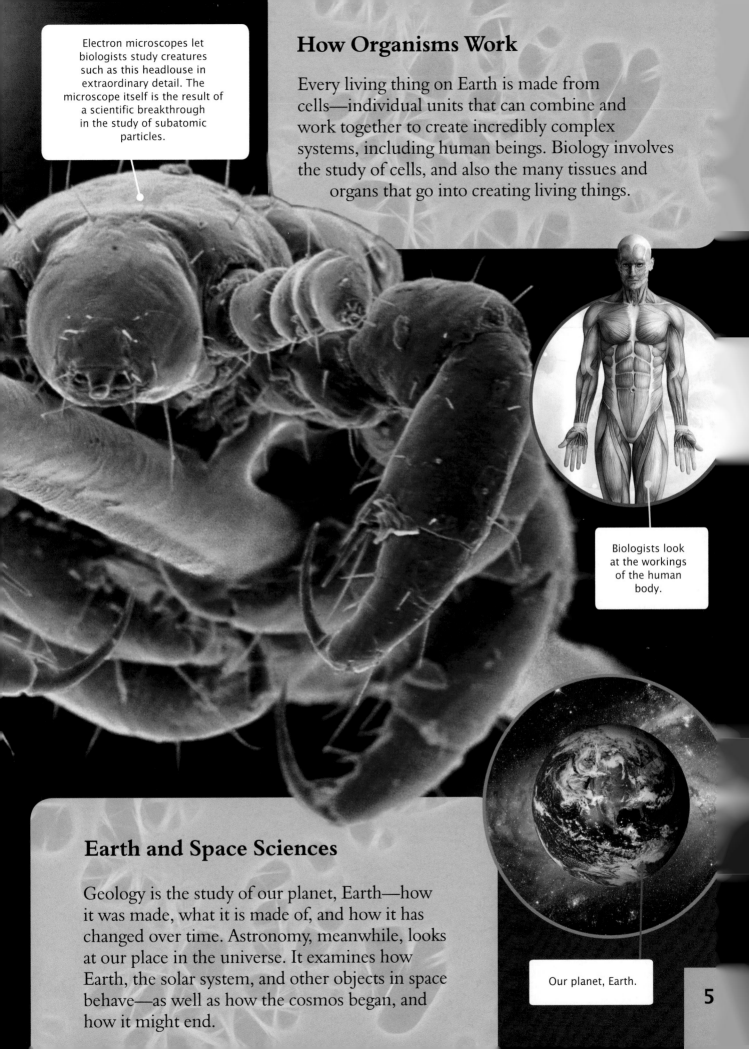

Electron microscopes let biologists study creatures such as this headlouse in extraordinary detail. The microscope itself is the result of a scientific breakthrough in the study of subatomic particles.

How Organisms Work

Every living thing on Earth is made from cells—individual units that can combine and work together to create incredibly complex systems, including human beings. Biology involves the study of cells, and also the many tissues and organs that go into creating living things.

Biologists look at the workings of the human body.

Earth and Space Sciences

Geology is the study of our planet, Earth—how it was made, what it is made of, and how it has changed over time. Astronomy, meanwhile, looks at our place in the universe. It examines how Earth, the solar system, and other objects in space behave—as well as how the cosmos began, and how it might end.

Our planet, Earth.

Physics Is Everywhere

Physics tells us that the velocity or speed of the rocket will depend on its mass.

Physics is the science that explains the workings of everything in the universe, from the tiniest to the largest scales. Its rules guide all the other branches of science, and we can see them at work everywhere in the world around us.

Understanding physics helps us build amazing machines. We can achieve tasks as complex as launching rockets into space.

Forces and Work

We're all influenced by forces. Gravity pulls things toward the ground, while friction slows objects down when they rub together. Without forces, nothing in the universe would ever change. A force can alter an object's speed, change its direction, or even change its shape. When a force applied to an object moves the object, that is called work. Work changes energy from one form to another or transfers energy from one object to another.

A man uses a pulling force to move the basket forward. The chemical energy in his body changes into kinetic, or movement, energy.

Other forces work on the basket, too: friction (resistance from the ground) and gravity (see pages 10–11).

AMAZING DISCOVERY

Scientist: Galileo Galilei
Discovery: Principle of relativity
Date: 1632
The story: Italian scientist Galileo's principle of relativity says it's not possible to tell whether you're on a body moving at a constant speed or a body that's not moving at all. He was thinking about whether the Earth revolves around the Sun or the Sun around the Earth.

The speed needed to escape Earth's gravity is called escape velocity. It is about 25,020 mph (40,270 kph).

The rocket keeps speeding up as long as the force pushing it up (thrust) is greater than the forces pulling it down (gravity and drag).

Made to Measure

Forces are measured in units called newtons. When we hold a 2.2-lb (1-kg) bag of sugar, we feel a downward force of almost 10 newtons thanks to the pull of gravity. Work is measured in joules. When a force of 1 newton moves an object 3.3 ft (1 m), the work done is 1 joule.

To work out the overall forward force on this speedboat, take away the drag or friction force created by pushing through the water from the thrust force made by the engine.

Newton's Laws of Motion

Scientist Isaac Newton laid the foundations of modern physics with three laws of motion that he identified in the late 1600s. These laws describe the way that objects move, how they react to each other, and how forces can affect their motion.

First and Second Laws

Newton's first law says that objects will always stay still or keep moving with the same velocity (speed in one direction) unless they are affected by a force. His second law states that the bigger that force on the object, the greater the change in its momentum. Momentum is an object's mass times its velocity.

When the downward force of gravity acts on the rollercoaster, it changes its momentum.

This cheetah weighs about 163 lb (74 kg), but the bull weighs ten times as much. The cheetah has a top speed or velocity five times faster than the bull, but it still has only half of its momentum.

AMAZING DISCOVERY

Scientist: Isaac Newton
Discovery: Laws of motion
Date: 1679–1687
The story: Philosopher Newton wanted to understand the elongated orbits of comets around the Sun. He realized they were obeying simple laws of motion—they were being influenced by the powerful force of the Sun's gravity.

According to Newton's first law, an object stays as it is unless a force acts on it. The force that gets the rollercoaster started is provided by the mechanical chain that pulls it to its first high point.

The downward stretches of the rollercoaster ride demonstrate Newton's second law. The mass of the cars and riders combines with the force of gravity to make the cars speed up down the track.

As the riders push down on their seats, the seats push back at them in an equal and opposite reaction.

Action and Reaction

Newton's third law of motion is that an object reacts to the force acting on it. The force of this reaction is equal to the original force, but in the opposite direction. If the masses of the two objects are the same, they push away from each other at the same velocity.

When a heavy bat applies force to a lightweight ball, it boosts the ball to high velocity. The bat recoils with a much lower velocity. The velocities aren't equal because the bat and ball have different masses.

Gravity

Gravity pulls skydivers down. When their parachutes open, the force of friction will slow their fall.

Gravity is the force that keeps our planet going around the Sun and keeps our feet on the ground. It is a force of attraction between objects with mass. Between small masses, it's too weak to notice. Between larger objects, gravity is so powerful that it can stretch across space and affect the shape the universe.

The Everyday Force

Isaac Newton was the first person to suggest that the same force which makes an apple fall from a tree also keeps the Moon in orbit around the Earth. He noticed that objects with a larger mass had more gravitational pull. If two objects both have large mass, then the force between them is even stronger. However, the strength of an object's gravity gradually gets weaker as you move farther away.

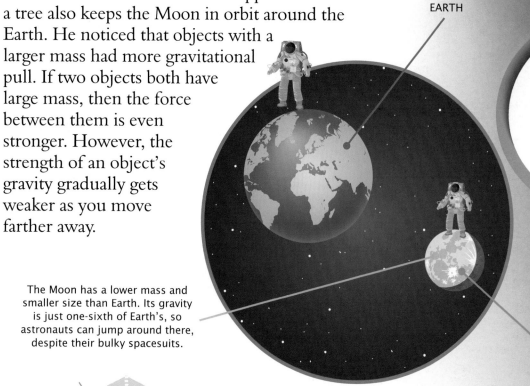

EARTH

Gravity is pulling the aircraft toward the Earth, but its wings create a lifting force to stop it falling.

The Moon has a lower mass and smaller size than Earth. Its gravity is just one-sixth of Earth's, so astronauts can jump around there, despite their bulky spacesuits.

MOON

AMAZING DISCOVERY

Scientists: Robert Hooke, Isaac Newton (left)
Discovery: Universal gravitation
Date: 1666–1687
The story: Newton's rival Hooke was the first to suggest that all massive objects produce a gravitational field that stretches away into space. Newton showed that this could explain the curving orbits of planets.

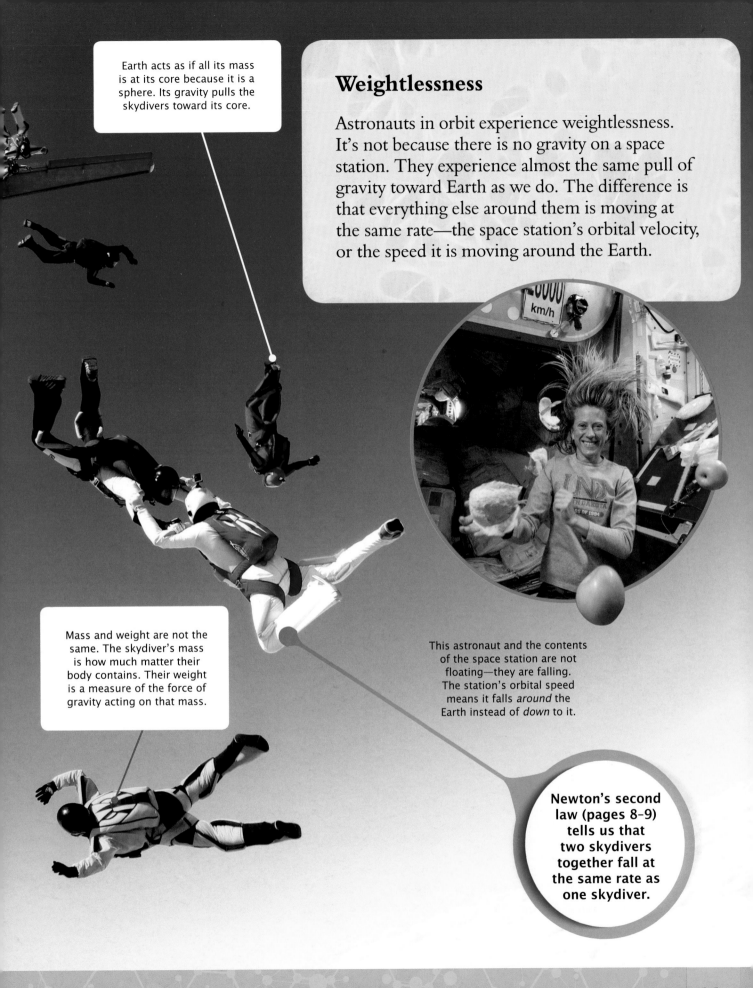

Earth acts as if all its mass is at its core because it is a sphere. Its gravity pulls the skydivers toward its core.

Weightlessness

Astronauts in orbit experience weightlessness. It's not because there is no gravity on a space station. They experience almost the same pull of gravity toward Earth as we do. The difference is that everything else around them is moving at the same rate—the space station's orbital velocity, or the speed it is moving around the Earth.

Mass and weight are not the same. The skydiver's mass is how much matter their body contains. Their weight is a measure of the force of gravity acting on that mass.

This astronaut and the contents of the space station are not floating—they are falling. The station's orbital speed means it falls *around* the Earth instead of *down* to it.

Newton's second law (pages 8–9) tells us that two skydivers together fall at the same rate as one skydiver.

Waves

A wave is a disturbance that transfers energy or movement in a particular direction. Waves are everywhere in physics. The most familiar types in everyday life are water and sound waves.

Measuring Waves

There are three ways to measure a wave: wavelength, frequency, and amplitude. Wavelength is the distance from one peak of the wave disturbance to the next. Frequency is the number of peaks passing a single point each second. A wave's overall speed is equal to its wavelength times its frequency. Amplitude is the strength of the wave disturbance itself.

Ripples spread out from the spot where the stone hit the water. These are waves and they are carrying energy. Ocean waves carry energy, too.

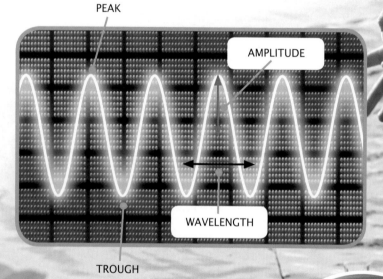

PEAK

AMPLITUDE

WAVELENGTH

TROUGH

When two waves meet, their effects add up. The waves get stronger where they line up neatly, but disappear where they don't—an effect called interference.

The ripples are evenly spaced. Each one is a separate, circular wavefront.

Scientist: Christiaan Huygens
Discovery: Huygens' principle
Date: 1678
The story: Dutch mathematician Huygens was the first person to describe how light moves in the form of waves. He also suggested that at every point on the front of the light wave tiny wavelets spread out in all directions.

These water waves are transverse. They're carrying energy across the surface as they move up and down.

Wave Properties

There are two main types of wave: transverse and longitudinal. Each has a wavelength, frequency, and amplitude, but each moves in a different way. Nearly all waves need a material to carry them, a substance called a medium.

WAVE MOVES UP AND DOWN

DIRECTION OF TRAVEL →

TRANSVERSE WAVES (eg light)
Transverse waves move in S-shaped waves. They vibrate up and down at right angles to the direction of travel.

WAVE MOVES BACK AND FORTH

DIRECTION OF TRAVEL →

MEDIUM COMPRESSED

MEDIUM SPREAD OUT

LONGITUDINAL WAVES (eg sound)
Longitudinal waves move in straight lines. They vibrate back and forward along the direction of travel.

Heat and Energy

Energy is the ability to do work and make things happen. Energy cannot be created or destroyed, but is always changing from one form to another. Heat is a form of energy that makes the individual atoms in a material vibrate or jostle around. Other types of energy often get "lost" as heat, and then can't be recovered.

Forms of Energy

Energy can take many forms. Moving objects have kinetic energy. Potential energy is energy that is stored and ready to be used to do work in the future. Chemical energy is released when bonds form in a chemical reaction.

Heat Transfer

There are three main ways that heat energy moves from one place to another. Conduction happens in solids. The energy travels from one atom to the next. Metals conduct heat better than wood. Convection happens in liquids and gases. It is a circular movement where hot areas expand and flow into cooler ones. Heat also travels as infrared (see page 20).

This is a Newton's cradle. The three balls on the right have no potential energy and no kinetic energy. The ball on the left has potential energy, because it has been lifted, but no kinetic energy. When the boy releases the ball, it will move and have kinetic energy.

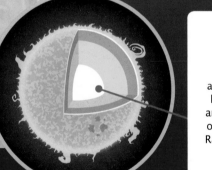

The Sun moves heat in all three ways. Conduction takes the energy from atom to atom. Convection makes hotter particles expand and rise to take the place of ones with less energy. Radiation carries the heat away into space.

AMAZING DISCOVERY

Scientists: Sadi Carnot and others
Discovery: Entropy
Date: 1824–1897
The story: In the 1800s engineers and physicists discovered that it's impossible to move energy from one form to another without losing some, often as heat. The lost energy can no longer do useful work, a state called entropy.

A single flash of lightning releases around five billion joules of energy.

Lightning heats the surrounding air to temperatures of more than 48,632°F (27,000°C).

A lightning strike has four main types of energy: electrical energy, heat, light, and sound.

Electricity and Magnetism

The flow of electric current and a magnet's ability to pick up metal objects may look like very different things, but they're both aspects of a single force—electromagnetism. They both generate force fields that attract objects or push them away.

Electromagnetism at Work

Any object with electric charge generates an electromagnetic field around it, which attracts objects with the opposite charge, and repels those with the same charge. A changing electromagnetic field, meanwhile, can cause an electric current to move through a conducting material.

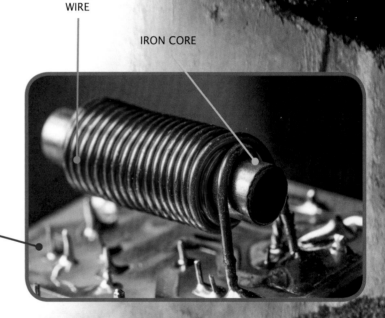

COILED WIRE

IRON CORE

In this simple electromagnet, electric current flows through a coiled wire to produce the magnetic field. The iron core in the middle of the coil makes the magnetic force more powerful.

AMAZING DISCOVERY

Scientist: Michael Faraday
Discovery: Electromagnetic induction
Date: 1831
The story: Faraday discovered induction while experimenting with wire coils on opposite sides of an iron ring. Passing current through one coil briefly magnetized the iron, and the changing magnetic field caused a brief current to flow in the other coil.

This huge electromagnet's job is to move sponge iron, a form of iron ore that is used in the steel industry.

The electromagnet's magnetic field is stronger than gravity so it can lift the sponge iron.

When the electromagnet is above the place where the sponge iron is needed, its current will be turned off. It will no longer be magnetic, so the sponge iron will drop to the floor.

Magnets

The power of magnets to attract and repel metal objects has been known for around 3,000 years. A magnet is surrounded by an invisible area that has special properties. This is its magnetic field. The strength and direction of the magnetic effect is different at different spots in the field. The magnetic pull is strongest nearest to the magnet.

The metals iron and steel are magnetic materials.

Iron filings scattered around a magnet line up with the magnetic field around it. All magnets have two poles. These are named north and south to match the magnetic field of Earth itself.

Secrets of Light

Light is a form of energy that travels as a series of tiny waves. Most of our light comes from the Sun or from electric lights. It moves extremely fast—in fact, nothing in the universe can travel faster than the speed of light.

Seeing Light

Light is a mix of wavelengths, which our eyes see as different hues. Red light has the longest wavelengths, and blue and violet have the shortest. A red T-shirt looks red because dye molecules in the fabric absorb light of all hues other than red, and only red light is reflecting back.

At night, when light from the Sun does not reach us, we use artificial electric lighting. The first electric street lights were invented in 1875.

What we see as white light is made up of many hues. When white light passes through a prism, we can see this visible spectrum, which has blue and red at opposite ends.

AMAZING DISCOVERY

Scientist: Isaac Newton
Discovery: The spectrum of visible light
Date: 1672
The story: Newton split a beam of sunlight into a spectrum (rainbow) using a prism, and then brought that spectrum back together to form white light. He showed for the first time that the prism was not somehow "adding" the different hues to light.

Tricks with Light

Light travels in a straight line from its source and bounces off objects (which lets us see them). Microscopes and telescopes use lenses to refract (bend) light and mirrors to reflect it. They can gather more light than our eyes alone, and also produce magnified images.

A magnifying glass bends the paths of light rays coming from the words. It creates a closer and larger virtual version of the words.

Neon lights are tubes containing neon, an element that is a gas. When electricity passes through the gas, it gives off light in a particular hue.

The light is behind this tree, which means the area in front of the tree will be in shadow.

Lights make our cities safer, but they also stop us from being able to see the night sky.

Invisible Rays

Visible light is just one type of electromagnetic radiation. It has a narrow range of wavelengths that our eyes can detect. Beyond it, there are other forms of radiation that are invisible to us. They carry energy from objects much hotter or colder than those that give off visible light.

Electromagnetic Spectrum

Radio waves have the longest wavelengths and come from the coolest, lowest-energy objects. We use them for broadcasting and for radio telescopes. Microwaves are next along the spectrum. We use them to send cellphone signals. Infrared radiation is produced by anything warm. Next comes visible light. Finally there are ultraviolet (UV) radiation, X-rays, and super-energetic, short-wavelength gamma rays.

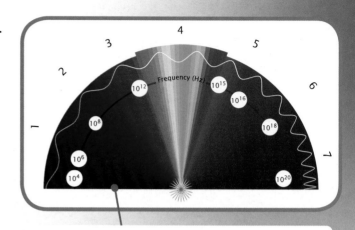

The different types of radiation are divided into a spectrum from long waves that carry little energy to short ones that carry lots. Visible light is just a small part of this electromagnetic spectrum.

RADIATION TYPES
1. RADIO WAVE
2. MICROWAVE
3. INFRARED
4. VISIBLE LIGHT
5. ULTRAVIOLET (UV)
6. X-RAY
7. GAMMA RAY

Rays in Action

The view from Earth's telescopes is distorted by our atmosphere, which is why stars twinkle. Space telescopes can give astronomers a clearer view. As well as visible rays, they collect invisible rays, such as infrared, X-rays, and gamma rays from stars and other objects.

Infrared telescopes use protective shields to block the Sun, and cold gas to cool their instruments. This lets them see weak rays coming from cool dust and gas in space.

Scientist: William Herschel
Discovery: Infrared radiation
Date: 1800
The story: Astronomer Herschel passed light through a prism and took the temperature of each hue. Just past the red part of the spectrum, where there was no visible light, he found the temperature was even higher. He realized there must be a type of light there that we can't see. He called it infrared.

Radiation from the Sun covers the whole electromagnetic spectrum, from radio waves to gamma rays.

The body produces heat that radiates out as infrared. Protective clothing stops this heat from escaping into the atmosphere and being lost.

Goggles shield this mountaineer's eyes from harmful UV radiation from the Sun.

Hidden Forces

Four fundamental forces are responsible for every type of interaction and relationship involving matter in the universe. Two of these, gravity and electromagnetism, work across large distances. The other two are much stronger, but are only felt on the tiny scale of particles inside the atomic nucleus.

Protons collide in special detector chambers. They are moving at 99.9 percent the speed of light.

The Large Hadron Collider (LHC) in Switzerland is the world's most powerful particle accelerator. It smashes particles together at high speed to find the building blocks of all matter, and the forces that control them.

Two beams of billions of protons shoot through the collider in opposite directions.

AMAZING DISCOVERY

Scientists: Shin'ichirō Tomonaga, Julian Schwinger, Richard Feynman
Discovery: Quantum electrodynamics
Date: 1947–1950
The story: These physicists explained the action of electromagnetism as a rapid exchange of "messenger" particles called gauge bosons, which carried force between normal matter particles. Since then, others have used the same idea to describe the two nuclear forces.

Nuclear Forces

The two forces inside the nucleus are called strong and weak (though the weak force is only weak compared to the strong one!). The strong force bonds particles called quarks to make protons and neutrons, and also holds those protons and neutrons together. The weak force can transform one kind of quark into another.

In a particle collision, the strong nuclear force works to bond them together. Its effect is stronger than the electromagnetic force that repels positively charged protons from each other.

B23R2

The beams travel around a 16.8-mile (27-km) circular tunnel.

Four Forces or One?

The four forces seem very different, but physicists believe that at least three (electromagnetism and the nuclear forces) work the same way. These forces also behave similarly in high-energy subatomic collisions such as those created at the LHC. Physicists suspect that all four forces were once united in a single "superforce."

STRONG NUCLEAR FORCE

ELECTROMAGNETIC FORCE

WEAK NUCLEAR FORCE

GRAVITY

TIME AFTER BIG BANG

The superforce existed very briefly in the early universe, where there was even more energy than in the LHC. Then the forces split from each other, but they kept certain similarities.

Einstein's Universe

Newton's laws of gravity and motion describe most of physics in the everyday world, but they break down in some extreme situations. In the early 1900s, Albert Einstein came up with an idea called relativity that offered a more accurate picture of how the universe really works.

This illustration shows how the masses of the Earth and the Moon change the shape of space-time. Distortion by the Earth is greater because it has a larger mass.

EARTH

This matrix represents space and time. For Einstein, these were aspects of the same thing.

Einstein said that matter makes space curve and causes light rays to bend.

Earth's gravity is distorting the fabric of space-time.

Special and General Relativity

Einstein's special theory of relativity (1905) describes how physics changes when objects travel at speeds close to the speed of light. His general theory (1915) sets out how physics behaves in situations with extreme gravity. Einstein explained that space has a structure that can be warped out of shape by large masses.

Distortions of space-time caused by large masses such as Earth hold smaller ones like the Moon in orbit around them

Blue light from a distant galaxy has its path changed as it passes nearer galaxies (yellow) that are bending space around them. The light reaches Earth as a series of distorted images.

Proofs of Relativity

The ideas of special and general relativity have been proved in many experiments. Special relativity causes clocks carried on fast-moving satellites to run more slowly than those that remain on Earth. General relativity explains how large masses can deflect the path of light that passes close to them.

AMAZING DISCOVERY

Scientist: Arthur Eddington
Discovery: Gravitational lensing
Date: 1919
The story: By photographing a total solar eclipse (when the Moon briefly hides the disc of the Sun), Eddington showed how the Sun's gravity deflects the path of starlight, proving Einstein's theory of general relativity.

Fun Facts

Now that you have discovered lots about forces and energy, boost your knowledge further with these 10 quick facts!

At take-off, the space shuttle's main engines produced 1.86 million newtons of force to lift the spacecraft against the pull of Earth's gravity.

Newton's second law explains why objects of different masses fall at the same rate—Earth's gravity makes them speed up at a rate of 32.2 ft (9.8 m) per second, every second.

Objects called black holes have such strong gravity that nothing can ever move fast enough to escape them—not even light!

Sound, a longitudinal wave, travels 1,125 ft (343 m) per second at a temperature of 68°F (20°C). Light waves, which are transverse, travel almost a million times faster.

At -459.67°F (-273.15°C), all atoms stop moving and have no kinetic energy. This is the lowest possible temperature, called absolute zero.

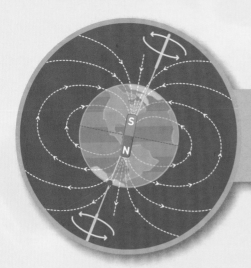

Every few hundred thousand years, the direction of Earth's magnetic field reverses completely.

Light travels at 186,000 miles (299,793 km) per second—that's fast enough to reach the Moon in around 1.3 seconds

Radio waves have the lowest frequency in the electromagnetic spectrum and the longest wavelengths—more than 62 miles (100 km).

Each proton circles the LHC track more than 11,000 times a second—the equivalent of a trip to Neptune and back—before it collides with ones coming the other way.

Astronauts on a six-month mission to the International Space Station age about 0.007 seconds less than if they stayed on Earth because of their orbital speed.

Your Questions Answered

We know an incredible amount about the forces and energy that affect the universe. But there is always more to discover. Scientists are still researching how forces are influencing even the tiniest particles and bonds, and are continuing to find out more incredible details. Here are some questions about forces and energy that can help you understand more about this vast and fascinating topic.

How do LEDs work?

Light emitting diodes, or LEDs for short, are a source of light, powered by electricity. Unlike "traditional" lightbulbs, which emit light from a vacuum or a gas (such as neon), LEDs emit light from a solid material. The diode is a semiconductor, which means it has a limited ability to conduct electricity. The light is produced when the electrons move around in the semiconductor.

How is "zero gravity" created for astronaut training?

In order to introduce astronauts to the sensation of weightlessness, many space agencies carry out training in "zero gravity" planes. These aircraft travel through the air by flying steeply upward at high speed, then dipping the plane's nose and descending. This downward flight results in the passengers falling at the same rate as the plane, briefly creating the sensation of weightlessness.

NASA training on a "zero gravity" plane. The sensation of weightlessness lasts for about 20–30 seconds

Why is UV light harmful to humans?

The Sun radiates two kinds of UV light, both of which are very energetic and have short wavelengths. UV-A radiation is both helpful and harmful to humans—it helps the body produce Vitamin D, but it also causes sunburn, which damages the skin. UV-B radiation reaches the cells of the body and can harm the molecules of the DNA. The body has developed responses that help repair damage, but they are limited and depend on the level of UV-B exposure.

How do maglev trains work?

"Maglev" is short for "magnetic levitation," and is just that— magnetism, used to levitate objects, in this case trains. The track is made of strong electromagnets, and the train levitates above it with the help of further electromagnets. Both sets of electromagnets have the same pole facing each other, so they repell and keep the train above the tracks. In order to move forward, the poles of the track's electromagnet are constantly switched, both "pulling" the train along the track, and keeping it in its levitated state.

Maglev trains can reach speeds of up to 375 mph (600 km/h).

Which energy is released during a nuclear explosion?

Nuclear explosions are vastly more powerful than even the largest "conventional" ones. Energy is released in different forms, the main one of which is blast energy— essentially a huge pressure wave moving outward form the explosion. Thermal energy sums up the heat and light that are released at incredible rates. A smaller proportion of the energy released is in the form of radiation.

The radiation energy released with a nuclear explosion continues long after the explosion has taken place.

Glossary

amplitude The maximum extent of a wave, measured from its mid-point to its trough or crest.

current The flow of electricity.

deflect To cause something to change direction.

DNA Short for Deoxyribonucleic Acid, the chemical ingredient that forms genes. Parents pass on copied parts of their DNA to their children so that some of their traits (like height and hair type) are also passed on.

frequency The rate at which something occurs over a certain amount of time.

generate To produce or create.

graviational pull The force of attraction toward something as a result of gravity.

induction The production of an electric or magnetic state through the proximity of an electric or magnetised object.

kinetic energy Energy that a body has because it is moving.

mass The amount of matter a body contains.

matrix A grid-like structure.

medium The material that a wave is moving through, such as air or water.

nucleus The positively charged core of an atom.

proton A subatomic particle with a positive electric charge.

radiation The release of energy.

revolve To move around an object in a circular pattern; to orbit.

thrust The force that drives an object forward.

velocity The speed of an object in one direction.

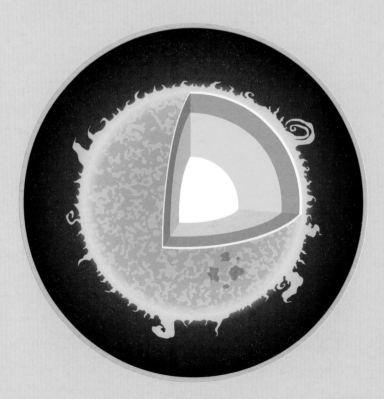

Further Information

BOOKS

Arnold, Nick. *Horrible Science: Killer Energy.* London, UK: Scholastic, 2009.

Arnold, Nick, and Kristyna Baczynski. *STEM Quest: Fantastic Forces and Incredible Machines.* Hauppauge, NY: Barron's Educational Series, 2018.

Davies, Kate and Adam Larkum. *What's Physics All About?* London, UK: Usborne, 2013.

Rowell, Rebecca and Venetia Dean. *Super Science Infographics: Forces and Motion.* Minneapolis, MN: Lerner, 2015.

Macaulay, David, and Neil Ardley. *The Way Things Work Now.* London, UK: DK Children, 2016.

WEBSITES

BBC Bitesize Energy
https://www.bbc.com/education/topics/zc3g87h
Explore this BBC webpage and find out much more about different forms of energy.

PBS Kids Design Squad
http://pbskids.org/designsquad/parentseducators/resources/index.html?category =forceenergy
Head to PBS Kids and discover lots of videos and activities to do with forces and energy.

Physics for Kids
https://www.ducksters.com/science/physics/
Visit this webpage to explore forces, energy, and many other physics topics, then test your knowledge with a physics crossword!

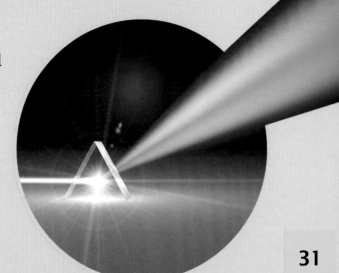

Index

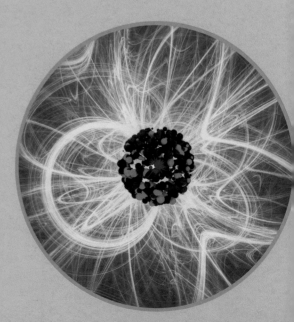